WHO EATS WHAT?

PRAIRIE
FOOD CHAINS

by Rebecca Pettiford

pogo

Ideas for Parents and Teachers

Pogo Books let children practice reading informational text while introducing them to nonfiction features such as headings, labels, sidebars, maps, and diagrams, as well as a table of contents, glossary, and index.

Carefully leveled text with a strong photo match offers early fluent readers the support they need to succeed.

Before Reading

- "Walk" through the book and point out the various nonfiction features. Ask the student what purpose each feature serves.
- Look at the glossary together. Read and discuss the words.

Read the Book

- Have the child read the book independently.
- Invite him or her to list questions that arise from reading.

After Reading

- Discuss the child's questions. Talk about how he or she might find answers to those questions.
- Prompt the child to think more. Ask: What other prairie animals and plants do you know about? What food chains do you think they are a part of?

Pogo Books are published by Jump!
5357 Penn Avenue South
Minneapolis, MN 55419
www.jumplibrary.com

Library of Congress Cataloging-in-Publication Data

Pettiford, Rebecca, author.
 Prairie food chains / by Rebecca Pettiford.
    pages cm. – (Who eats what?)
 Summary: "Vibrant photographs and carefully leveled text introduce readers to the prairie biome and the food chains that operate there. Includes picture glossary and index" – Provided by publisher.
 Audience: Ages 5-8.
 Audience: K to grade 3.
 Includes bibliographical references and index.
 ISBN 978-1-62031-303-9 (hardcover : alk. paper) – ISBN 978-1-62496-355-1 (ebook)
 1. Prairie ecology–Juvenile literature. 2. Food chains (Ecology)–Juvenile literature. 3. Prairie animals–Juvenile literature. I. Title.
 QH541.5.P7P48 2016
 577.4'4–dc23

                                    2015027082

Series Editor: Jenny Fretland VanVoorst
Series Designer: Anna Peterson
Photo Researcher: Anna Peterson

Photo Credits: All photos by Shutterstock except: Alamy, 19; Getty, 14-15, 20-21b; iStock, 9, 16-17; Nature Picture Library, 20-21b; Thinkstock, 18.

Printed in the United States of America at Corporate Graphics in North Mankato, Minnesota.

TABLE OF CONTENTS

CHAPTER 1
Land of Grass.................................4

CHAPTER 2
The Prairie Food Chain....................8

CHAPTER 3
Food Chain Close-Ups 18

ACTIVITIES & TOOLS
Try This!......................................22
Glossary 23
Index...24
To Learn More..............................24

CHAPTER 1

LAND OF GRASS

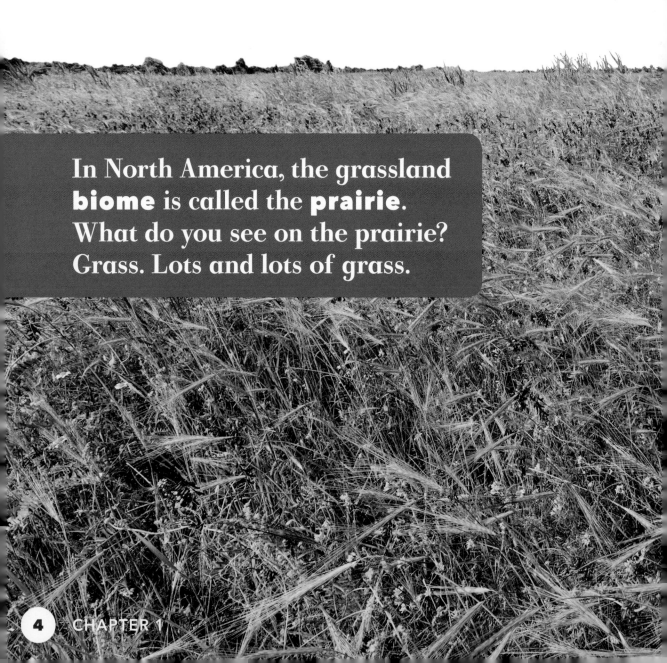

In North America, the grassland **biome** is called the **prairie**. What do you see on the prairie? Grass. Lots and lots of grass.

Some prairies have tall grass. Others have short grass. There are not many trees. Summers are hot and winters are cold. The soil is rich.

Fires keep a prairie healthy. They burn trees and other plants that might crowd out grasses. Ashes mix with the rich soil and help grasses grow.

Grass roots are long. When wildfires burn the grass, the roots survive. The grass grows back.

WHERE ARE THEY?

There are grasslands on almost every continent. The prairie in North America is called the Great Plains.

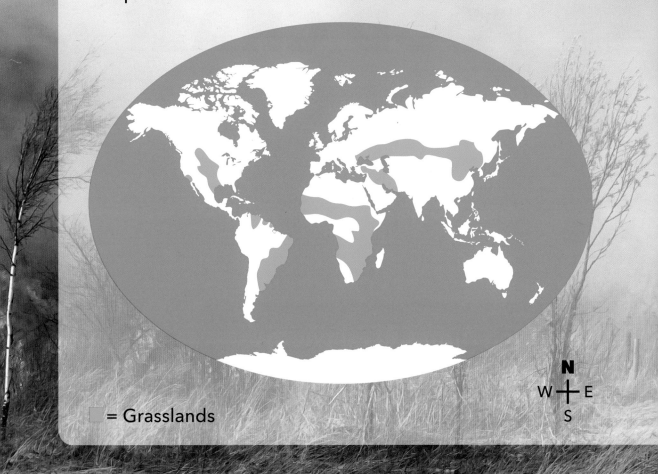

= Grasslands

N
W E
S

CHAPTER 2

THE PRAIRIE FOOD CHAIN

All living things need energy to grow and move. Plants get it from the sun, soil, and water. Animals eat.

A **food chain** shows what they eat. It starts with plants and ends with animals. Each living thing in the food chain eats the one before it.

Prairie grass and wildflowers are **producers**. These plants use energy from the sun, soil, and water to make their own food. They are the first link in the prairie food chain.

DID YOU KNOW?

A prairie gets 10 to 30 inches (25 to 76 centimeters) of rain each year. Too much rain would make it a forest. Too little would make it a desert.

Animals such as **rodents** and **bison** eat grass and other prairie plants. They are **consumers**, the next link in the chain.

DID YOU KNOW?

Prairie dogs are rodents. They dig vast underground homes called towns. Their digging adds air to the soil. This makes the grass stronger.

bison
(consumer)

garter snake
(predator)

coyote
(predator)

Animals such as falcons and coyotes are **predators**. They eat consumers. They are the next link in the food chain.

Large predators will also eat small predators. For example, a coyote will eat a snake.

DID YOU KNOW?

Farmers use rich prairie soil to grow food. But too much farming destroys the grassland. It puts the food chains at risk. This reduces the food supply, and many animals die. Today, people are planting **native** grass seed to rebuild the prairie.

When an animal dies, worms and insects break down its body. They are **decomposers**, the last link in the chain. They return nutrients from the dead matter to the soil. This helps plants grow.

TAKE A LOOK!

One prairie food chain might look something like this:

Producer:
Prairie Grass

Predator:
Fox

Consumer:
Prairie Dog

Decomposer:
Beetle

CHAPTER 3

FOOD CHAIN CLOSE-UPS

Let's look at a simple food chain.
Grass grows on the prairie.
A prairie dog eats the grass.

prairie dog
(consumer) ·····▶

badger
(predator)

A badger eats the prairie dog. In time, the badger dies. Worms break down its body. The nutrients make the soil rich. The food chain begins again.

Let's look at another food chain.

1) This one starts with prairie grass, too.

2) Then a **pronghorn** eats the grass.

3) A coyote eats the pronghorn.

4) When the coyote dies, beetles break down its body. The nutrients help new plants grow.

The food chain continues!

ACTIVITIES & TOOLS

PRAIRIE TAG

Play prairie tag with your friends! Your "prairie" can be a basketball court, a yard, or a driveway. You'll want six or more players.

❶ Two players are coyotes. Four or more players are prairie dogs.

❷ Coyotes stand in the middle of the prairie. Prairie dogs stand at one end of the prairie.

❸ Prairie dogs must run from one end of the prairie to the other. Coyotes try to tag (eat) as many prairie dogs as they can.

❹ If a coyote "eats" a prairie dog, the prairie dog must freeze. Prairie dogs that reach the other side are free!

❺ A tagged prairie dog becomes a coyote in the next game. (On a real prairie, coyotes often grow in number when they have plenty to eat.)

❻ If a coyote starves (does not tag anyone), he or she must be a prairie dog next time. (On a real prairie, there are more prairie dogs when there are fewer predators.)

GLOSSARY

biome: A large area on the earth defined by its weather, land, and the type of plants and animals that live there.

bison: A large ox that lives on the North American prairie.

consumers: Animals that eat plants.

decomposers: Life forms that break down dead matter.

food chain: An ordering of plants and animals in which each uses or eats the one before it for energy.

native: A plant or animal that grows or lives in a certain area.

prairie: The grassland biome in North America.

prairie dog: A ground squirrel that lives on the North American prairie.

predators: Animals that hunt and eat other animals.

producers: Plants that make their own food from the sun.

pronghorn: A deer-like animal that lives on the North American prairie.

rodents: Nibbling animals such as such as mice, squirrels, and prairie dogs.

INDEX

animals 8, 9, 12, 15, 16

biome 4

bison 12

consumers 12, 15

coyote 15, 20

decomposers 16

eating 8, 9, 12, 15, 18, 19, 20

energy 8, 11

farming 15

fire 6

grass 4, 5, 6, 11, 12, 15, 18, 20

insects 16

nutrients 16, 20

plants 6, 8, 9, 11, 12, 16, 20

prairie dogs 12, 18, 19

predators 15

producers 11

rodents 12

soil 5, 6, 8, 11, 12, 15, 16, 19

sun 8, 11

trees 5

water 8, 11

wildflowers 11

worms 16, 19

TO LEARN MORE

Learning more is as easy as 1, 2, 3.

1) Go to www.factsurfer.com

2) Enter "prairiefoodchains" into the search box.

3) Click the "Surf" to see a list of websites.

With factsurfer, finding more information is just a click away.